Benito Juárez

HERO OF MODERN MEXICO

Benito Juárez

HERO OF MODERN MEXICO

by Rae Bains
illustrated by Allen Davis

Troll Associates

Library of Congress Cataloging-in-Publication Data

Bains, Rae.
    Benito Juárez, hero of modern Mexico / by Rae Bains;
illustrated by Allen Davis.
        p.   cm.
    Summary: Describes the life of the Mexican president who
instituted many social reforms and led his country in a war of
independence.
    ISBN 0-8167-2825-9 (lib. bdg.)   ISBN 0-8167-2826-7 (pbk.)
    1. Juárez, Benito, 1806-1872. 2. Presidents—Mexico—Biography—
Juvenile literature. [1. Juárez, Benito, 1806-1872.
2. Presidents—Mexico.] I. Davis, Allen, ill. II. Title.
F1233.J9B35 1993
972'.07'092—dc20
  [B]   92-2291

Benito Juárez

HERO OF MODERN MEXICO

The first light of day crept over Mexico's Sierra del Sur mountains. The villagers of San Pablo Gualatao were still sleeping—except in the house of Marcelino and Brigida Juárez. Everyone there was awake, getting ready for an important event. The Juárezes' one-day-old son was to be baptized that very afternoon. It was March 22, 1806, and the baby was to be called Benito Pablo.

All was ready. Señor Juárez stood at the door, holding the sleeping baby. Maria Josefa and Rosa kissed their new brother. Señora Juárez stroked the baby's soft cheek. "We will wait for your return," she said to her husband. "Go with God."

That afternoon Benito Pablo Juárez was baptized at the tiny village church in Santo Tomas Ixtlan. The family had no money for a celebration or even for a new baby blanket. Señor Juárez gave a few coins—all the money he had—to the priest who baptized the baby.

The Juárezes felt lucky that they were able to do this much for their newborn. Most of the twenty families in their village had no money at all. The lives of everybody in San Pablo Gualatao were a constant struggle against poverty, starvation, and disease.

The Juárez family, like their neighbors, were Zapotec Indians. Their ancestors had lived in the mountains of southern Mexico for thousands of years. They were peace-loving, hard-working people who farmed the land and raised sheep.

When the Aztecs overran Mexico in the twelfth century, they found it difficult to conquer the Zapotecs. And when the Spanish *conquistadores* invaded Mexico in the sixteenth century, they met the same stubborn resistance.

The Zapotecs were not an aggressive people. They did not invade other peoples' territories. They simply defended their own land, and they never gave up. Benito Juárez was born into this tradition of pride, quiet strength, and the will to survive. It was this tradition that shaped his life. And it explains Juárez's importance to the shaping of modern Mexico.

Right from the start, life was hard for Benito. As he wrote when he was an adult, "I had the misfortune not to have known my parents... for I was hardly three years old when they died, leaving me and my sisters to the care of our paternal grandparents, Pedro Juárez and Justa Lopez, Indians also of the Zapotec nation."

Benito's mother had died giving birth to another child. There were no doctors or nurses in San Pablo Gualatao. His father had collapsed and died in a marketplace in the city of Oaxaca, after walking forty miles over the mountains from his village, carrying fruit grown in his small garden. Señor and Señora Juárez were not even thirty years old when they died.

When Benito was six, his grandparents also died. The three Juárez children were homeless again. Maria Josefa went to Oaxaca, to work as a housemaid. Rosa, who was in her teens, married and moved to a nearby village.

Benito was taken in by his father's brother, Bernardino. Bernardino Juárez owned a small plot of land in the mountains. It was near the Laguna Encantada, "the Enchanted Lake." Despite its name, there was nothing enchanting about the land. It was rocky and steep, with barely enough grass for Uncle Bernardino's small flock of sheep to graze on. Benito was put right to work. He did chores in the house, carried water from a nearby stream, and helped his uncle tend the flock.

Benito spoke only the Zapotec language. This was fine for talking with family and friends. But the official language of Mexico was Spanish. Without knowing Spanish, there was no way for a person to be anything but a poor peasant. But there were no schools in any of the Zapotec villages. The lack of education made it almost impossible for a person to break the chains of poverty.

"Our people have lived in this land for thousands of years," Uncle Bernardino told the boy. "Even so, we remain poor and without opportunity. You are smart and learn fast. You must use what God has given you and make your life better. You must learn Spanish. You must learn to read and write. You can be somebody special, Benito. You must not live out your life as a poor uneducated man!"

Bernardino Juárez wanted Benito to become a priest. He said that was the best way for a poor Zapotec boy to get ahead in the world. But to be a priest, the boy had to go to a seminary. And to be accepted by the seminary, Benito had to learn Spanish.

Uncle Bernardino knew a little Spanish, and tried to teach it to his nephew. Benito wanted to learn. But it wasn't easy. It took endless hours of work just to survive. Everything the family needed came from their own efforts. Their clothing was made of cloth they wove themselves. The cloth came from thread they spun themselves. And the thread came from the wool of their own sheep.

Every bite of food the Juárezes ate—bananas, prickly pears, brown beans, potatoes, chickpeas—came from their own garden. They ground their own flour to make tortillas. They harvested honey from their own beehives. Nothing was bought, not even the tools they used to farm the land.

Benito Juárez never forgot what life was like during his childhood. Some years the crops failed, and times were especially hard. Then the family had to survive on a cactus plant called maguey, which grew in the rocky soil. The sap of the maguey was like sugar water. It tasted sweet and was nourishing to the body.

The Juárezes drank the maguey sap and used the rest of the plant in many other ways. They made thread, called pita, from the fibers. The pita was made into sturdy cloth and paper. Even the thorns did not go to waste. They were used for pins, needles, and nails.

Young Benito and his family were exhausted by sundown, worn out by endless hours of work. There was little time left to learn Spanish, or anything else. Again and again, Bernardino told his nephew, "My greatest wish is for you to go to school, to escape this life. Maybe someday soon it will be possible."

But "someday" never seemed to come any closer for Benito. When he was ten years old, he was put in charge of his uncle's flock of sheep. The boy spent every day up in the hills overlooking the Enchanted Lake. Benito was lonely and unhappy. He passed the time talking to the sheep and dreaming of a better life.

There was only one way Benito could think of to escape the endless poverty and make something of his life. As he wrote many years later, "Fathers who could afford the schooling of their children took them to the city of Oaxaca for that purpose. Those who could not pay the fee put the children into service in private homes on condition that they be taught to read and write. This was the only method of education in use, not only in my village, but in the whole district of Ixtlan.

"It was a remarkable fact in that period that most of the servants in the houses in the City were young people from that district. Because of these facts . . . I came to the conclusion that only by going to the City could I learn, and I often begged my uncle to take me to the capital."

Uncle Bernardino always promised to do so, someday. But it was another "someday" that never came. And then, one day, everything changed.

It was December 16, 1818, and twelve-year-old Benito was up in the hills watching the flock. Around eleven o'clock that morning, a group of mule-drivers passed by on the road. Benito asked them if they came from Oaxaca, and they said they did. The boy had many questions about the big city. The men told him wonderful stories of the people, the buildings, and all the grand things that happened there. Then they continued on their journey.

When Benito went back to his flock, he noticed
that one of the sheep was missing. He scrambled
up and down the rocky paths, looking for the
lost sheep. Then, as he wrote, "Another shepherd
boy approached and told me that he had seen
one of the mule-drivers make away with the
sheep."

Benito felt stupid at being fooled by the slick-talking men. And he felt guilty for losing a valuable animal. Uncle Bernardino had so little, but he shared everything he owned. He always treated Benito like a son. The boy was also afraid of being punished. As he sat on the hillside, frightened and confused, Benito decided to run away. By sunset, as he led the flock home, he had a plan.

The next morning at dawn, Benito sneaked out of his uncle's hut and began walking to Oaxaca. It took all day to cover the forty miles, and he was hungry, thirsty, and tired when he finally reached the city. There he looked for the house of Don Antonio Maza. Maria Josefa, Benito's big sister, was a cook there. She was the only person he knew in the whole city, and he had to find her.

When at last Benito found the Maza house, he told his sister what had happened. She went to Don Antonio, repeated the boy's story, and asked that Benito be allowed to stay there. "My brother is strong and willing to work," Maria Josefa said. "He wants to stay in Oaxaca. He hopes to go to school. Will you help us?"

Don Antonio agreed to let Benito live in the house until the boy found a permanent place to stay. Benito earned his keep by doing odd jobs for the Maza family. When he was not working, the boy from the tiny mountain village roamed the streets of Oaxaca. He listened, looked, and learned.

Oaxaca's buildings and gardens were more beautiful than Benito ever imagined. There were marketplaces with endless varieties of vegetables, fruits, meats, cakes, furniture, silks, lace, and silver. Finely dressed people rode in horse-drawn carriages.

Before he came to Oaxaca, Benito had only known poor Zapotec Indians living in tiny villages. Now he began to see what other parts of Mexico were like. And what he saw was a Mexico ruled in a cruel way, a way unfair to most of the people. Half of all Mexicans were Native Americans, like the Zapotec. But they were treated more like animals. Mexico's Native Americans had no rights under the law. They had no education and no opportunity to improve their lives.

The next largest group of Mexicans was called *mestizo*. The *mestizos* were part Native American and part Spanish. *Mestizos* were treated better than Native Americans. But they, too, did not have a voice in the way Mexico was run.

Next there was a smaller group of people, called Creoles. The Creoles were descendants of Spanish people, but they were born in Mexico.

The smallest group in Mexico were people born in Spain. These people ruled Mexico, and they had more legal rights than anyone else. Mexican laws were so unfair that children born in Mexico to Spanish parents had fewer rights than their parents. For this reason, the laws often turned children and their parents into enemies.

When Benito was a boy, Mexico was still a colony of Spain. Many Mexicans hated Spain the same way the English colonists farther north hated England's rule. Those colonists had declared their independence from England in 1776, and gone on to become the United States of America. Mexicans suffering under the iron rule of Spain longed for the same freedom and independence.

Spain kept a stranglehold on Mexico with a code of strict laws. Mexicans were not allowed to make or grow anything that was made or grown in Spain. That meant machines, cloth, tools, and many other manufactured goods had to be bought from Spain. Among the many forbidden crops in Mexico were flax and hemp (used to make cloth and rope). Mexicans were not allowed to grow grapes, or the mulberry trees needed to feed silkworms that made silk. And every ounce of Mexico's greatest wealth—the millions of tons of gold and silver in the mountains—was shipped to Spain to fill the treasury of the Spanish kings.

Mexico received nothing in return for all this gold and silver. Even though there was no legal slavery in the country, most Mexicans lived like slaves, in total, hopeless poverty. This fueled a growing anger in the country. By the time Benito Juárez reached Oaxaca in 1818, there had been two revolts against the government. Both had been crushed by the army, but that only deepened the people's fury against their rulers.

Mexico was a troubled land when twelve-year-old Benito began his education. Don Antonio Maza had found him a place in the home of Don Antonio Salanueva. Don Antonio Salaneuva was a kind, intelligent man. He was deeply religious and believed that education was very important. So when his new houseboy, Benito, showed a strong desire to learn, Don Antonio enrolled him in an elementary school.

In the next two years, Benito went through four grades. He learned to read and write simple Spanish. Schools for Native Americans were allowed to teach basic subjects, but no more than that. Benito wanted to learn more, and he begged to be sent to a better school. Don Antonio agreed. He wanted Benito to become a priest, and that required a real education. So he sent the boy to the Royal School.

The Royal School was well known for educating young men, and Benito was excited to be a new student there. But he soon learned that the school had two separate sections—one for Native-American boys and one for Spanish and Creole boys. The Native-American class didn't even have a regular teacher. Instead, the class was taught by an untrained assistant. And when Benito or one of his classmates made a mistake, they were not helped, they were punished.

Years later, Benito Juárez remembered, "I was disgusted with this wretched method of instruction. Since there was no other establishment in the city to which I could go, I decided definitely to leave school, and to practice the little I had learned by myself, until I could express my ideas in writing."

True to his word, Benito spent many hours reading and teaching himself grammar, spelling, and penmanship. He studied late into the night in Don Antonio's library. Benito's life was not all work, however. He still found some time for fun and friends.

Benito and his friends liked to play running and jumping games in the neighborhood. The boys also found time for pranks, with Benito leading the way. Once, he bought a basket of rotten apples for a few pennies. He gave the apples to his friends to use as ammunition. Their target was anyone unlucky enough to be in the marketplace. When Don Antonio heard about this, he was furious and let Benito know it!

Another of Benito's ideas was more acceptable. At a nearby lakefront, he built a diving board, using a barrel and two wooden boards. The first time he tried jumping from it, Benito and the board went into the water together. The next time it worked, and Benito charged other divers to use it. At a few pennies a jump, he made enough to buy a huge bag of candy to share with all his friends.

On October 21, 1821, fifteen-year-old Benito entered the seminary in Oaxaca. Over the next four years he mastered Spanish and Latin. In August 1825, he passed his examinations with a grade of "Excellent." But Benito Juárez didn't stop there. He continued his studies at the seminary with advanced classes in philosophy, the arts, religion, and literature.

As Juárez studied more and more, a new plan took shape. Instead of becoming a priest, he decided to serve his people by becoming active in government. With this as his goal, Juárez finished his seminary studies and enrolled in law school at the Institute of Arts and Science in Oaxaca.

After three years of intensive schooling, Benito Juárez became an assistant professor at the Institute. He was also elected to the Oaxaca city council. This was the beginning of his political career.

The next year, 1832, Juárez was elected to the state legislature. His fame began to spread throughout the area. Juárez was admired for being thoughtful, hard-working, and honest. Most of all, he became known for supporting laws that were fair to *every* citizen, and for seeing that the laws were carried out.

Mexico was still in distress and confusion. The country had won its independence from Spain in 1821, but it wasn't truly free of Spanish control. There was a national legislature, and many state legislatures as well. Representatives to the national and state legislatures met, debated, and passed laws. But all the laws didn't change anything, because they didn't apply to the army, the church, and the ruling upper class.

Again and again, local heroes led rebellions against one state government or another. Each time, they were defeated. The Mexican people continued to suffer.

Some of the leaders of these rebellions were just political bosses who put together a ragtag army. Other were fanatics with dreams of glory and power. Still others were corrupt bullies or fast-talking con artists. There were a few leaders who had good intentions. But they had no practical way of making their wonderful promises come true.

Benito Juárez was not like any of these people. He wasn't a brilliant speaker or a glamorous figure. He always wore simple, dull clothing, not a colorful uniform with shiny buttons, ribbons, and decorations. He led no army and made no grand promises. Still, his fine reputation grew. As a lawyer and as a representative, he concentrated on what mattered most.

What, Juárez asked himself, do the people of the villages need? The answer was the chance to rise from poverty. They needed money to improve their farms, and a way to get their crops to other people.

Juárez believed that one of the key answers to the problems of Mexico was roads. The few roads that linked the villages were no better than muddy tracks filled with stones. Juárez wanted to improve the roads, so the villagers could get to the big cities and sell their crops.

Juárez also believed that Mexico needed a constitution that guaranteed equal rights for everyone under the law. And he favored a bill of rights similar to the one enjoyed by the citizens of the United States.

Throughout his life, Juárez fought hard for his ideals. At different times he served Mexico as Deputy to the National Congress, Minister of Justice, Governor of Oaxaca, Chief Justice, and Minister of the Interior. Finally, in 1861, Benito Juárez was elected President of Mexico. Even then, he and his wife, Margarita (one of the daughters of Don Antonio Maza, the man who had taken Benito into his home when he was a twelve-year-old runaway), lived simply in the presidential mansion.

Juárez's career wasn't a steady climb to success. There were times when he left government service entirely. It was his way of showing his disgust at the corrupt, criminal dictators who gained power. Twice, these dictators drove Juárez from Mexico because he refused to join their evil rule. The people loved and honored Juárez because of this, and welcomed him home each time he returned.

Benito Juárez was President of Mexico during the United States' Civil War. He was a great ally of Abraham Lincoln's government. Juárez hated all slavery, so he refused to trade with the Confederacy, even though it meant refusing money that Mexico badly needed. Doing the right thing was more important to Juárez than making money.

Some Mexican politicians had other ideas. They saw a way to gain great wealth and power by being allies of the Confederacy. They planned to set up an independent empire in northern Mexico and let the Confederate armies use it as a safe zone. Juárez's enemies told the Confederate leaders, "You will be free to attack the Union forces and then escape to this zone. The U.S. government will not be able to follow you over the border into Mexico. Crossing the border means going to war with Mexico and all our European allies. That is something President Lincoln will not do." Juárez's enemies also hoped this plan would give them enough power to overthrow President Juárez's constitutional government.

But Juárez, supported by the Mexican people, defeated the plotters, and Mexico remained a strong friend of President Lincoln. Lincoln was grateful to Juárez for helping the U.S. government at a critical time in its history.

Juárez remained President of Mexico until he died, in 1872. He had wanted to retire, but the people saw him as their best hope for honest government. They re-elected him again and again.

Through all the years he spent as president, Juárez never stopped trying to improve the lives of the poor and uneducated. He succeeded in having a railroad system built from the coast to Mexico's capital, Mexico City. He fought long and hard for a law guaranteeing a free education for every child. His reforms brought the chance for equality to all. Under Juárez, Mexico finally became an independent nation, with the power to decide its own destiny.

"Benito Juárez is Mexico and Mexico is Juárez," said Andres Iduarte, a famous Mexican writer. The poor Zapotec child from the hills grew up to become the living symbol of his country.

INDEX

		DATE DUE	